ACKNOWLEDGEMENT

I would like to thank God for the strength, clarity, and perseverance to complete this work. To my family and friends — thank you for your patience, encouragement, and belief in me even when I doubted myself.

To everyone who has faced fear, disappointment, or uncertainty and continued to press forward — this book is for you.

May these words inspire you to release what no longer serves you and step into the life you were meant to live.

SPECIAL ACKNOWLEDGEMENTS

Lynette Jemmott   **Wife**

For all the ways you inspired and
supported me.

Kevin Brown   **Pastor**

Thank for your spiritual leadership
and your unconditional friendship.

Damian Jean Baptiste   **Ministry
                                Leader
Your spiritual zeal and commitment   (Deceased)**
to advancing the Lords work and your
love for people.

Will Zanders   **Business
                                Mentor**
Your example of selflessness, wisdom
and inspiration makes us better.

Luis Molero   **Son/Author**

Your Zeal and Passion for life
continues to inspire all.

ABOUT THE AUTHOR

Deryck Jemmott is a motivational author, speaker, and entrepreneur dedicated to helping individuals break free from fear, limitation, and self-doubt. Through real-life reflection, faith-centered insight, and practical wisdom, Deryck challenges readers to confront the mental barriers that keep them from becoming who they were created to be.

With a passion for personal growth and purpose-driven living, his writing encourages readers to take responsibility for their lives, release the weight of the past, and step boldly into their potential. JUST LET GO is both a call to action and a reminder that greatness already exists within us, waiting to be unlocked.

CHAPTER ONE

JUST LET GO
of the
"I CAN'T" notion.

I can do all things through Christ who strengthens me - Philippians 4:13....

The Holy Bible

It is amazing in the Bible, the words "I can do all things"appears. It strengthens those who believe. Yes, those who believe it can make it happen. Remember when you were young, the one thing you thought you could not do, one day you summed up courage when no one else was around and tried it.

Sometimes we failed, more than once but armed with the thought," I think I can ", we persevered and then it happened, victory at last, we did it.

Now it was time to show others that we could get it done. What are we thinking that we can't get done now, are we not older, stronger (mentally and physically) and wiser than when we were children? Hold on to the all-consuming thought, "I can't ". There is nothing we can't achieve if we persist. It might take longer than we hoped or more tries than we anticipated, it may even cost us more than we bargained for.

But once we've done it there is no stopping where it will take us. So often, we hear or read about people who defy odds to succeed and we sigh. Sometimes we think "we can do that" other times we say to ourselves, "they are not that special" and worse "we had a similar idea".

What made them succeed when we are still sitting on our laurels? They decided to let go of the notion: "I can't". Is it that simple? Can we achieve our dreams and goals by simply letting go? It is that simple, but no one said it is easy.

Easy is for bums, lazy minded people who expect life owes them. We are not those types of people, we know that we can if we put the work in, if we face our fears and if we stick it out to the end. We are made to defy the odds to succeed in this life of chance. When the dice of life are rolled and it's not our number then we have another opportunity to fulfill our destiny and purpose.

However, life only gives us "X" number of chances, and we don't know what that number is. We just must make good with what we have till our number is played.

Every day we are faced with the opportunity to change our present and the chance to shape our future. This will only happen when we let go of the notion: "I can't". What can't we do?

 Let's see, we can't run a 100-meter race in less than 10 seconds, but we can run 100 meters. We can remember hearing the saying, "the race is not for the swift but for the ones who make it to the end". (my paraphrase) We've heard the story of the tortoise and the Hare.

We are not as fast as the Hare, but if we remain focused and steady and just keep on going on, we will reach the end and enjoy the benefits of our efforts. For some it will take a few months or other it will take years, but for all of us it will happen once we just let go, because we know we can.

The question we now ask ourselves is: "When will we let go?" Will it take an "ah- ha" moment like losing our job or home or some loved one?

We all seem to float in the lake of "I can't ", until life forces us to swim. Suddenly we realize what good swimmers, in fact we are even greater swimmers than we imagined.

The only way to know is when we let go and trust in our instincts, in that feeling that is knurling at the core of our bones. Some call it intuition, others inspiration but we all have it and we've all felt it at one time or another, maybe we are feeling it even now. What will we do about it? Well reality is, we can ignore it or accept it. If we ignore it, we will continue to float in the lake of "what if", maybe buy a boat for more safety and security.

We will continue to live life, but there will always be a void and gaping hole of un-fulfillment and we will tell ourselves, 'It's okay', or 'it wasn't meant for us', or we will lull ourselves to sleep with the pacifying notion that 'it's not our time'.

However, if we accept it, we will jump into the lake of "what ifs" and kick and struggle as we swim to the shore of opportunity. As we reach it, we will look back, fulfilled and contented that we did all we could to make it and guess what, we made it!

We must stop rating our success by someone else' success, just celebrate our success. We did it! We have succeeded in whatever way no matter how small or how great.

We've done it and we are no longer bound by the notion "I can't" in the lake of "what ifs". We now live on the shores of opportunity, fueled by the thoughts of "I can" yes that's right "I can do all things".

CHAPTER TWO

JUST LET GO
of the
"FEAR" that cripples.

"The only thing we have to fear is fear itself"

– Franklin D Roosevelt

On March 4, 1933, newly elected U.S. President, Franklin D Roosevelt, uttered the now famous words, "the only thing we have to fear is fear itself" during his inaugural speech. The United States was facing one of the worst economic crises in history, people had a lot to be afraid of; the unknown, the country's economic future and what the future held for them. Strange as it seems we fast forward to present day, and we face the same fear of over 80 years ago.

The eternally optimistic President Roosevelt did try his best to keep the country from erupting in panic. Maybe it was that statement or one of his innovative new approaches that kick started the economy, whichever things began to rapidly improve soon after that speech.

Roosevelt realized that "Fear" was formless and faceless as it creeps into the core of our beings and cripples us from even trying.

The fear of drowning prevents us from enjoying our beaches and swimming pools. The fear of flying keeps us from travelling the world. Daily, we face our biggest fear – the fear of the unknown and it has its talons embedded deep within our souls. We are kept in the same place to go to jobs, with the same we are ok friends. Security in the form of Jobs stability (for the record we are all expendable).

We have been here 20 years on the job, we have ok savings, they match 4% or 5% of our 401K contribution. So, we don't rock the boat, soon we will retire and live on half our current income (which barely fulfils our current needs), unlike our colleague that was just let go. (Company is downsizing or AI taking over).

We have been approached by all types of people to join one networking scheme after another or we have an idea that would improve everyone's way of life. But it's not for us because the fear of the unknown...the what ifs...the I don't know...etc. What if it works for you, what if you were born to be an entrepreneur, to build an empire, to create new things or motivate others.

Over 80 years ago, President Roosevelt helped us realize that we have nothing to fear. Fear only exists if we give it a foothold. Entrepreneurs sprung up and faced the unknown as a result the luxuries we enjoy today are the result of them letting go of their fears. What are we holding back from the next generation?

What are we preventing from coming to be? Are we still being held back by fear, namely the fear of the unknown? Go to a mirror and look straight into the eyes of the one looking back at you. Can you see the fear in their eyes; it's not the unknown that we fear. The fact is it's the known we fear, it's the person looking back at us in the mirror, the same person who judges our every move and questions the existence of our very being.

Our greatest fear is not formless and faceless as President Roosevelt thought our greatest fear looks back at us daily, when we wash our face or brush our teeth. Our greatest fear is us. Get radical smash that mirror (not literally) and shatter the fear that has its talons in you. Release the awesomeness the world needs and waits for from us.

Experience the power of knowing that we control our fears and our fears don't control us. Sometimes that fear has a physical form and face like that of a spouse. The fear of disappointing them keeps us from taking risk swimming out into the unknown and we opt for comfort and safety. Every so often you must confront that fear, don't go smashing this one like the one in the mirror.

Sit down and discuss, explain and enlighten, we usually need to build up the courage to do this, but just let go of the "I can't" notion and you are halfway there. We have a plaque we bought at crafts fair years ago it says: "I live with fear and danger every day; occasionally I leave her and go fishing". We get the drift sometimes we must leave the fears behind and go out there and bring home "the catch of the day".

Fear lives within the empty craters and fills them with anxiety, inadequateness, shame and doubt. It grows to be gigantic, the more we let it fill the craters of our minds and soul. So, we fill our craters with positive things; "more than conquerors" thoughts "yes, we can" sayings and we give life to fearlessness. It defeats fear because it knows that fear is formless and faceless, and it needs us to exist.

We on the other hand don't need fear to exist, we were born to rise above the odds, to face fear and defeat it. To vanquish it and become victorious is in our DNA. President Roosevelt was right "the only thing we have to fear is fear itself". It is not that scary after all once we accept it.

CHAPTER THREE

JUST LET GO
of the
"I AM NOT GOOD ENOUGH"

We all have days where we feel inadequate, when nothing seems to be working for us. At work our colleagues seem to excel and we are stuck on the plane of mediocrity. The ability to reach the same level as others is like climbing Mount Everest. All we see is no matter how hard we try there's no getting out of this plane, as we are being left behind.

We see our school mates moving ahead, they own their home and even a vacation home, they drive new luxury cars, vacation in exotic places and we still rent and drive that 10-year-old clunker, our vacation is 3 days off at home barbecuing in the backyard.

When will we get a break? When will we get ahead? It seems every time we move one step forward; we take two steps backward. If this is all we will see, the clouds surrounding Mount Everest that have blocked the sun, so our future looks dark and bleak.

Yet around us we see everyone else being successful. We often look at others for the measure of who we are. How far we can go and what we can do, finally we judge our lives by the successes of others.

As though they have the measuring stick as to what standards we need to live to. We sit and ponder about all the external material niceties we see other people with.

Only if we could be smart enough to go to college and get a degree, or could sing like that, or have $100,000.00 a year plus salary, even a family like them. Stop it! Are we not tired of the "woe is me or poor little me routine"? We are not good enough, smart enough, worthy enough, and talented enough and the list goes on and on and on.

Remember we are the sum of all our fears, the sooner we accept that we have nothing to fear than fear itself, the sooner Mount Everest as insurmountable as it seems becomes a hill that with a little more effort the easier it is to climb.

That's right, what is Mount Everest? We can climb it, we are children of the universe, not just some of us, all of us and we have the same right to pursue happiness as the next person.

No one can take that away from us, but we can give it away so often we throw it away and get caught up in the "woe is me" syndrome. Daily we hear on the news of those who are in a worse predicament than us, we hear but we don't internalize.

As 'horrible' as our lives seem there must be at least ten people looking at our lives hoping theirs will get as good as ours, and for them at least another ten wishing theirs will be as good as those looking at us and so on and so on. We live our lives for us with the right to pursue happiness.

 Happiness can't be bought or sold, don't get it wrong money can - with the emphasis on can - make it easier, not all ways better. When we read about Lottery winners or people who come into millions but still are unhappy, we usually say to ourselves that wouldn't be us.

When they were just like us, we were waiting for the chance, the opportunity or the right time. The acquisition of wealth will only magnify who we are: if we are selfish, our selfishness shows more,if frivolous with money now, the more frivolous we will become then.

If our happiness comes from material things, then we will just add and add, but never be satisfied with all we accumulated.

When we are at peace with all we have and continue to appreciate all we have, then and only then will the clouds move from the mountains in our lives. The sun will illuminate and cause the 'gems' in our lives, - that we have taken for granted- to shine.

Not only will we wake up, but we will get up, we will face each day with determination, with purpose and we will strive for more. We know we are worth far more than we thought, we no longer must wait to achieve but we can achieve and become all that we can be. We have a right to be here as much as the trees and the stars. We are the children of the universe and makers of our own destiny.

We cannot make someone else's destiny come to be and no one can make ours happen. We are and we will be all we are meant to be. We are not measured by anyone's standards; we create the standard and we will not let fear or inadequateness keep us back. We will press forward with the privilege of being a precious child of the universe.

CHAPTER FOUR

JUST LET GO
of the
"NEGATIVE NUANCES"

"Once you replace negative thoughts with positive ones, you'll start having positive results".

-Willie Nelson

We all have experienced starting the day with vigor and optimism; we notice the dew on the grass, the budding of the spring flowers, and the falling of autumn leaves even the cool fresh crispness in the air. Today will be different, we have a new attitude, nothing will steal our joy, not our family, the neighbors not even our boss. Nothing, no one will steal our joy, so life just back away, this our day.

Then it happens, someone makes fun of us or our abilities, we feel the awkward darkness of negativity creeping in. We are stronger than it – the darkness – it will not win, we will not let it win, but it's there and it is not going away. Here comes another negative thought: maybe, they are right, we can't shake it- the negativity. Then it changes, we smell it - the stench, it fills our noses, overcomes our sense of reasoning, and diminishes the brightness of the day.

We just can't shake it, now everything and everyone seems negative and we lose it. We become just as negative as those around us. Why did we not just walk away? Shun the nuances and enjoy the freedom of our new-found positivity.

That is all it took, walk away and laugh, laugh at the thought that something or someone could spoil the day. Then we take a moment for ourselves, breathe. That's right breathe, take a deep breath straighten our shoulders, now exhale not only the air we breathe in but the stress and negative thoughts that were inside. Read that special piece of poetry or prose, listen to your favorite song, think about the times things were better and hold that feeling, look at the future and see that things will only get better.

A wise man once said that when you are in the valley the only way out is up. So, take courage though we seem to be in the valley of despair there is only one place to go from here – UP. So, let's muster the faith and strength needed to climb what seems like an insurmountable mountain and accept that yes, we can and start to climb.

Never let discouragement get to you, remember we are children of the universe with a right to be here. So do not forget it or the rights we have, it is time to exercise those rights starting with choice.

We have the rights of choice – Choose not to stay in the same valley for too long; choose to be free of the shackles that bind us financially; choose to be better today than yesterday; choose to be strong; choose to move on; that right CHOOSE!!!

Letting go of negative thoughts and emotions is not easy, but just like everything in our lives it can be learnt. The skill or ability to let go can be harnessed and even mastered with practice. First to let go we first acknowledge that it is negative, and it will take us to that dark place. It will lead us down a path of self-destruction that will affect all those around us and pull them into the vortex of fear and despair.

Next, we write down or say the opposite of what we are feeling or experiencing now.

If we feel, then write or say

When we feel:

SAD then say I am GLAD

ANGRY then say I am CALM

AFRAID then say I am COURAGEOUS

POOR then say I am RICH

TIRED then say I am ENERGIZED

Repeat it as many times as necessary so soon we will be in the POSITIVE frame of mind that will produce positive results in our lives. Oh, and always remember to smile.

CHAPTER FIVE

JUST LET GO
of the
"PAST"

'We are products of our past, but we don't have to be prisoners of it.'

- Rick Warren

"The Purpose Driven Life" by Rick Warrewn points out that growing up we are shaped and influenced by those in people in our lives. They are meant to guide us, nurture us, and give us the will to succeed at whatever we put our minds on. Sometimes, they do a great job of raising us and our awareness; sometimes, they do a not-so-great job. So, what, we are grown now, and we make our own decisions.

We chisel our own paths in the rock of Life; we can decide to let our past shape our futures or like so many that have gone before us, we can use our present to channel our energies to create the future we deserve. We have all heard of the great athletes, entertainers, actors who came from less than desirable surroundings; they stayed focused and with unstoppable determination.

They took the 'Rock' that life handed them and forged a glorious future. Though it did not happen overnight, it did not take thousands of years like it takes 'Rock' to become a diamond (else they would've died before making it big). It will however take heat and pressure to create something new out of the ordinary, the result, a precious gemstone.

It will be so for us all unless you find your fairy godmother (let's not live in a fantasy world). We face the heat of opposition which we first must learn to bear, followed by the pressure of disappointments and finally the length of time to become what we have always imagined. Most of us survive the heat and pressure but we tend to give up before our time.

So, what if we had a tough childhood? What if everyone said we will not be or do anything significant? Our parents called us dumb or stupid for the silly things we did growing up. Our teachers felt we were not college material and hence gave us little attention. Our school grades were not above average, so we were labeled as slow or average.

We all have something we excel at whether it be sports, drama, cooking, gardening, building or demolishing, or even creating things. We are harmony with it is our Zen – a place of retreat, place of self-worth. It is here we find peace and fulfillment. We tend to coward towards this place and regroup when life throws it's all at us instead of using it to move forward, we seem to retreat and move backwards.

Teachers felt we were not college material and hence gave us little attention. Our school grades were not above average, so we were labeled as slow or average.

We all have something we excel at whether it be sports, drama, cooking, gardening, building or demolishing, or even creating things. We are harmony with it is our Zen – a place of retreat, place of self-worth. It is here we find peace and fulfillment. We tend to coward towards this place and regroup when life throws it's all at us instead of using it to move forward, we seem to retreat and move backwards.

Deep inside lies the fear that they may be right, so it prevents us from pressing forward to what we believe deep within our cores. Instead of going after what we are destined for; instead of activating the inert gift that was placed inside of us from birth; we keep it hidden from the world. If we were all Lawyers, Doctors, Architects or Engineers where would the great movies or music come from? Where would the amazing meals or works of art be.

There would be no variety to spice life up, we would live in a mundane world – a world without color or expression. Accept this simple fact; our past has no effect on our future unless we let it.

We can change the direction in which our lives are going by realizing that we have the tools, skills and abilities to make a difference in the world or at least in our community. As children, we all had dreams that were eroded away by life's heat and pressure over time. It's time to stop and break free of what we think and think new thoughts just like when we were younger thoughts of 'We will be all that we can be ', because it's the true we can be all that we were meant be. We will no longer live out the template that life has drawn out for us, we will become the artist with the blank canvas – the canvas of life.

We will paint with the colors of our choosing and in so doing create our own masterpiece, our own work of art, yes, we will create our lives the way we want and be contented with all it has in store for us. We will be free to live, to love, and to pursue happiness: - our happiness, in a future not shaped by our past but chiseled out of our present.

CHAPTER SIX

**JUST LET GO
of the
"COMFORT BLANKET"**

Linus is almost never without his blue security blanket which debuted in the June 1, 1954, strip.

- Charles M. Schulz's Peanuts comic strip…

Hey Linus, it's time to put that blanket away! So often we act like Linus, we have our security blankets – those things we are comfortable doing and we never deviate from them. For some of us it's our careers, others it's our looks, others our friends and family, whatever it is we hold on tightly and don't ever want to let go.

We become so comfortable in our jobs and careers that provide our homes, cars, and luxuries of life - even though we are unhappy. "It's not what we went to college to do but it pays the bills" we so often say. "We don't get to see our families as much, but we provide everything they need, that's why we work so much". One day we must find the time and sit down with our significant other and our children and ask this question: "Is there anything you would rather have than all that I have provided?" The answer will probably surprise us "More time with you".

What are we doing about it? Usually nothing, the mortgage and car notes must be paid, don't be reckless but consider the alternatives how about pursuing that passion that's inside being smothered by our security blanket -the job. Are we not pursuing happiness in every area of our lives? How do we go about pursuing it?

Is it possible to be truly happy in all areas of life?

If we are in the field of our dreams, then we will be contented and that's where happiness starts. We will find that all the areas in our lives begin to align and our security blanket is no longer our careers but has been replaced by the passion of excellence and the desire for something bigger than we are. However, if we are not in the field of our dreams, we are constantly faced with strife and issues, we are discontented, and our lives seemingly begin to unravel. We are unhappy with most areas of our lives and find solace and comfort in our security blankets.

Like Linus we hold our blankets to our faces to cover the reality of what's going. As we bury ourselves deeper in its comfort, we excuse ourselves from taking responsibility for the reality that's our world. Finally, it shatters when we pull our blankets from our faces with utter amazement as to where things are at, then quickly return it to our faces and continue in the security it offers. Some of us were blessed with the security blanket of beauty. Everything we have was predicated by our looks.

We find that life is easy, everyone loves us, we are pleasing to the eye. Then people get to know the real you, that is not as beautiful on the inside as the exterior implied. Suddenly we are surrounded by a host of admirers, usually out of envy or jealousy or those who use us as entry to places they normally would not have access to.

We are taught use the good looks God gave us to get ahead, and while there is nothing wrong with that philosophy, we should always remember what was said about fame and beauty in Ezekiel 16:15: "But you thought your fame and beauty were your own. ..... Your beauty was theirs for the asking."

Be aware that beauty and fame last for a season then the security of the blanket diminishes with time and becomes worn and develops holes with age.

We need to let our beauty shine from within by using our talents and minds and step out of our comfort zone to create a better and brighter world. So, as our security blankets become ragged and torn with age, let the legacy we leave with our lives with live on forever, always bright and beautiful. We know that true beauty comes from the inside but use our external beauty not as our security blanket but as the base to build real security that lasts.

CHAPTER SEVEN

***JUST LET GO
of the
"DOUBT"***

"Doubt can only be removed by action."

- Johann Wolfgang Von Goethe

Let's face it doubt has plagued our lives at some point or another but somehow, we overcame it. Growing up we all saw the older kids riding bicycles and it looked like so much fun. We persuaded Mom or Dad or both that all we wanted for Christmas or our Birthday was a bicycle. On receiving it our eyes lit up like large moon shaped lights, there were squeals of joy we finally got what we wanted.

Then the reality soon hit there was more to riding a bicycle than what meets the eye. At first, we peddled shakily with the assurance that once Mom or Dad held the back of the seat or training wheels were on, we were safe.

See even back then we doubted that we could ride without assistance and when that assistance was not present, we stared at the bicycle as though it had grown horns and its only mission was to throw us off like the bull at the bull ring. Something inside of us pressed us to get on and try one more time. In many cases we fell, got bruised, but got back on the ferocious bull we now call "bicycle". We were determined to conquer it no matter how many times we fell this was our bicycle, other conquered theirs we will conquer ours. Shortly afterwards we found ourselves speeding, making jumps, twists and turns on our bicycles and years later we are still confident we can ride.

This brings us to the truth about our present-day lives. We have dreams and goals we want to accomplish be it Being our own boss, losing weight, living in a nicer zip code, finding the one to spend the rest of our lives with and on and on. For each of us it is different, yet the same as we face the daily ups and downs, falls and spills to the point they become unfathomable and unreachable dreams and goals just like when we were young.

Life seems to grow horns determined to undermine all our efforts to make it. Few get back up and try again, most of us slink away into a corner and look at our dreams as fantasy: - good to look at never to be enjoyed. Waking up is the only way we accomplish our goals by defeating doubt. See ourselves as more than able be willing to fall and get back up.

Kobe Bryant is one of the world's best basketball players (in my biased opinion he's the best). He didn't start out that way, in his early years when his team needed him most he sucked (for the lack of a better word).

Kobe did not let that stop him. No, he practiced hard, he did what other ballers weren't doing for longer until he became better. He no longer doubted that he could make the basket when it counted, even if it was from the other side of the court. His actions off the court removed his doubt on the court.

Today, we can remove the doubt that enshrouds us by the actions we take. It's not rocket science to lose weight simply eat less and exercise more. To find that person to love, become a person to love. To move into that zip code, increase your income. To be your own boss learn how to be a great employee, then apply those principles to your own business.

We diminish doubt by our activity off the court like Kobe. For that raise or promotion, we put in the extra hours without grumbling or complaining, trust me the powers that be will see your efforts. Losing weight is all about being disciplined not at the dinner table or family events but when we are on the court by ourselves watching what we eat.

Finding love this is tricky: as men want a woman to love and respect us but do we set a standard of Love and respect for her to see and follow. Women want to be loved and have security in the relationship but are they loving and respectful so that a man would love them back and build a secure life with them.

We can all achieve all that we want, just let go of the doubt and replace it with action or simply let your actions, despite the doubt you have lead you. Eventually you will overcome doubt, sooner than you think and will be riding the wave of success jumping, with twist and turns like a professional. Like the day we learnt to ride our bicycles, doubt will never have control over that area of our lives again.

CHAPTER EIGHT

JUST LET GO
of the
"DISTRACTIONS"

"It's hard to stay true to yourself and what you want in life when there are so many distractions and so much craziness going on around you".

-Hilary Duff

They are all around us, set in place to hold back the weak minded, they give the appearance of being useful, but the reality is they are void of purpose and true fulfillment. They are our distractions, for each of us they are as different as the seashells on the seashore. Some are small decorative, others medium ideal for collecting while occasionally there are large decorative, collectable and functional shells - like the conch shell that you can blow.

However, when we look at them, they are all shells just like in our lives they are all distractions. So, what has been holding us back from accomplishing that thing we are meant to do? We can all justify (excuse) why we are not where we want to be in life. Everyone one knows life can be hard, yet some of us break through the barriers that hold our destiny and others do not.

Is it that they are better equipped than us, last time I checked they had the same two hands and two feet; the same two eyes and ears; and the same one mind and one mouth? Is it that life is hard or is that inherently we are lazy not willing to use what God gave us to its fullest.

Instead, we look around and deem that those who are succeeding got a lucky break or found the favor of someone's eyes? Reality is they just wanted it a little bit more, saw it a little clearer and became laser focus on achieving it, so they got rid of the distractions. The television show or game became less important to acquiring success just like the friends who just want to party and have fun but broke before pay day.

We must look in the mirror and be truthful to ourselves; ask the question: What or who is holding me back? The answer is: - if we are being entirely truthful it is always the same - ME! We are right; Life is hard and the greater the distractions the harder it gets.

So, what distractions we must let go, for each of us it is hard, but no-one ever said the path to success is easy. Though not easy it is do-able, others have done so and moved on to a better life, others are currently doing it with our brave faces on smiling as we go through the hurt and pain of change.

Now is the time, once we realize who is holding us back; ourselves the path to our destiny becomes clear, take a deep breath put on our big-boy pants and just let go of the distractions.

Life distractions can have serious strongholds on us, many of us need help letting go so we surround ourselves with like-minded people – not necessarily with the same dream as ours – with a mindset to let go of the distractions to get all that life has to offer. We can ask for help as we journey together keeping each other accountable to make it.

CHAPTER NINE

JUST LET GO
of the
"SLAVE MENTALITY"

"I freed a thousand slaves, I could have freed a thousand more if only they knew they were slaves"

- Harriet Tubman

In 1981, Mauritania became the last country in the world to abolish slavery, when a presidential decree abolished the practice. However, no criminal laws were passed to enforce the ban. In 2007, "under international pressure", the government passed a law allowing slave holders to be prosecuted.

It is amazing we Live in America which abolished slavery in 1865 or even England which abolished slavery in 1833 but sometimes we still act like we are in Mauritania an Islamic country one of the largest counties in Northeast Africa trying to keep slavery alive here in the United Staes of America.

Slavery may be gone, or is it? We simply found a way to rename it and replace it. Practically put have we dressed it up and re-package and re-banded it, so it became appealing to the public but held the same values as in the days of slavery? Did life replaced the Plantations with Corporations? When we pause to look at the structure of both, there is an uncanny similarity dress in modern flora.

PLANTATION	Vs	CORPORATION
Slaves start and finish work at the time assigned by the Master		Employees clock in/out based on our employer time schedule
Slaves were branded to denote which plantation they belong		Employees get badges & /or uniforms to indicate their company
Loyal Slaves were elevated to Field Masters and House servants		Loyal Employees get promoted to Supervisors and Managers
Field Masters and House Servants all report to the Master on what is happening with the other slaves and quality of work		Supervisors and Managers, all report to the CEO on what is happening with the other employees and quality of work
Masters provides Food, Lodging and Clothing based on one's position		CEO pays a salary based on position, that determines where we live, the foods we eat and clothes we wear
Created fear of running away by treatment and punishment		Keeps Employees with 'Benefits Packages' so they won't leave.

Today we get all caught up in Jobs and careers and become slaves to someone else dream. Our hard work furbishes lavish lifestyles for our CEOs, leaving us to dream that one day it will be us. Only to come to the realization 40 years later and 40% of your income, to live on. We can barely make it so we end up with secondary jobs to cover living expenses.

We should have broken free and live life on our terms, building our own legacy for our families. As crazy as it sounds, we are still enslaved mentally, and do not even know it. So many of us are afraid to leave the Plantation (job) and venture out, afraid to invest in us and our abilities.

No matter how many opportunities present themselves to us. Fear of losing the 'shackles' of benefits, prevents us from trying business opportunities despite evidence of their soundness.

Enslaved to this is "too good to be true", "We can't live like the Master". So, we will continue to slave for our companies till they put us out to pasture – Retirement is the modern-day word for you are longer useful to us. Someone once said: "Insanity is doing the same thing and expecting different results".

Well, "Slavery is working the same dead-end job and expecting Financial Freedom". Are we the slaves that are free or the ones that still don't know we are slaves?

The decision is made based on our next steps. Not saying we quit our jobs, but saying, seek multiple sources of income and use the plantation oops, - I meant – corporation, to our advantage like the smart slaves we 'be' that are free.

CHAPTER TEN

JUST LET GO
of
"OURSELVES"

"Our deepest fear is not that we are inadequate. Our deepest fear is that we are powerful beyond measure. It is our light, not our darkness that most frightens us"

–Marianne Williamson

What do we really fear? So often when asked why people don't own their own businesses, the responses are swift: We do not have enough knowledge; We do not have the financial ability; We are afraid of venturing into the unknown; We are afraid of failing. Are these really the true reasons?

As we examine them more closely, they all have the same root cause – that lies in us. When we say: "We do not have enough Knowledge" we forget the internet, Siri and Google between the three of them, we can amass the knowledge to move ourselves forward. We can find the necessary resource materials and even learn from others. Have you ever heard... YouTube-it? (Look it up in Youtube).

Constantly we are amazed that everything we think of doing instructions can be found on You-Tube. Google gives us so much information it makes our heads spin, but the same way it can be posted on the internet with our due diligence we can find what we need. It seems that we hold ourselves back from exploring and applying the knowledge that is within our grasp to build whatever our minds can conceive.

"We do not have the financial ability" Did Banks or Credit Unions close? So, what our credit is not the best, what steps are we making to improve it? Are we even trying to figure out how to make it better or are we holding on to it, so as not to change it?

There are so many ways to raise funds for our projects if we just put ourselves out there. GO FUND ME and even CASH APP and FACEBOOK.

It is funny we post our fake realities on Facebook, Instagram, Snap Chat and other social media platforms, rather than expressing our true dreams and goals. We want others to see us as successful, having fun and lacking nothing. For once dispel the façade and post what our heart's desire and ask others to join us on the quest.

We will be surprised by two things of the hundreds of friends on our social media that claim they are living the lie – meant Life really are broke without two pennies to rub together and so cannot help you really, but they will give us a 'thumbs up' or a 'like'. Then you will be surprised at those who are really your friends and those that are not.

See, we surround ourselves with ourselves and then wonder why we are not better. A wise man once said if you are in a group of five people, four are broke be assured we will be the fifth broke person in the group. Being comfortable around people like us will not stretch us and cause us to grow.

So be the broke person in a group of 5 wealthy people, guaranteed we will be the next wealthy one. "We are afraid of venturing into the unknown" – Stop it!

We are conditioned our whole lives to deal with the unknown – from Kindergarten to Middle school; from Middle school to High school; from High school to College/Work; from College to Work; from one Job to another Job; from Interns to Staff; from Staff to Supervisor; from Supervisor to Assistant Manager and so on we get the drift. Each stage of our lives has equipped us, or we equipped ourselves to be better.

It is the same thing in our life cycle from Babies to Toddlers; from Toddlers to Kids; from Kids to Pre-teens; from Pre-teens to Teenagers from Teenagers to Young Adults; from Young Adults to Adults; from Adults to Middle Age; from Middle age to Retired.

We learn to deal with all the changes that occur in between birth and death whether it being a new parent to becoming a seasoned on or a first-time grandparent to the greatest grandparent of them all each stage was new and unknown.

Yet we faced it with steadfastness and reliance to make it through nothing has changed other than we took the unknown and made it our own. Finally, "We are afraid of Failing" Are we afraid or do we tell ourselves that so we can sleep at night in the cesspool of our mediocrity and wake smelling like roses.

If by reading this, we are not convinced that we have succeeded at the most important thing of all – LIFE, we can put this book down and crawl back into the dark, cold, distorted reality of our lives and finish out our days on earth. Snap out of it. We have made it so far; we are awesome do you know how many thousands did not get this far and wished they could have. We are magnificent, smart beautiful people it is time we let the world know that we are here to stay and to make a difference.

Step out of our darkness and let our light be shed abroad, the world is waiting on us, our families are waiting on us, our friends are waiting on us. When we shine for others to see they will in turn believe and start to shine as well and collectively we will make this a better world for us all to live in.

CHAPTER ELEVEN

JUST LET GO
of
"PEOPLE AND THEIR OPINIONS"

"Care about what other people think and you will always be their prisoner."

— Lao Tzu

In today's world where social media denotes who we are, we are drawn into people's lives and must measure up to what our friends are saying or doing. Constantly being bombarded with daily posts and the feeling we do not measure up. Afraid to venture out on our own dreams and ideas, - scared of what people think or say. Wake up! They are talking about it anyhow. If you try something new you are a fool, if you do not you are still a fool.

Once we understand that insanity is doing the same thing and expecting a different result. Crazy is being bothered about what people think. It is your dream not theirs so put on blinders like the ones put on horses, so they only see what is in front of them. Dig your heels in and go after it.

Failure does not mean you have failed - simply failure is only failure when we stop trying. Where would we be if Benjamin Franklin gave up on his first or tenth time creating the lightbulb or who would the know of Abraham Lincoln if he never persisted in dream of being President of the United States.

Success is achieved by a series of failures (or as we now know it as a series of 'not yets'). Let them snare and joke about your dreams, never be ashamed by those who don't dream or fear going after their dreams.

Do not publicize dreams or goals on Facebook, TikTok or Instagram for people's approval instead tread daily one foot in front the other repeatedly. Success is waiting around the corner if you do not stop stepping and moving forward. Its timing is not determined by you but the consistency and determination of your efforts.

Be assured you will win, you will reap a harvest if you fail not just keep going and later you will quell the opinions. Know who you are and let no one imprison you with their limitations. Life is too short not to at least try to achieve your dreams and goals.

Reach out for help it just might take a village to birth and raise your baby (dream). Seeking out mentorship from those who have done it, you will find the ones who are willing to help.

Most of all seek out God, learn to trust him and listen to voice. In the Bible he says, "But seek first his kingdom and righteousness, and all these things will be given to you as well." Matthew 6:33 NIV

As we close learn to listen to what God says about you not man. Trust that he has a purpose and plan for your life. As it unfolds it will drastically change your course, but as you trust his guidance be assured God's plan is to give you hope and a future.

So, focus on the dream God puts inside you and block out the opinions of others. Just let go and go live your best life yet.

www.ingramcontent.com/pod-product-compliance
Lightning Source LLC
Chambersburg PA
CBHW041104110426
42740CB00043B/150